This workbook belongs to:

_____

DESCRIPTIVE WRITING TASKS WITH HELP SHEETS

This book contains help for 20 different examples of creative writing tasks typically found in English language exams. These exam question examples all follow the same style:

Write a description of …… as suggested by this picture…

Remember to use these suggestions as a starting point and let your creativity guide you while writing. It is crucial to have a clear structure and compelling language to engage the reader. Planning is an essential part of the descriptive writing process – look at the sections of information provided as prompts to help kick start your planning and ideas.

You are advised to spend 45 minutes for each of these example exam questions.
Write in full sentences and you should also plan your answer.
You should leave enough time to check through your work.
This section is worth 40 marks.

Smartstart Online: 07508933571, message for information about private tuition sessions online.

Planning help:

Write a description as suggested by this picture:

Think!

Viewpoint will have a dramatic effect on your descriptive writing – should only happen over a period of 5-10 seconds otherwise it becomes a NARRATIVE, a story, this is a description not a story!

Point of View:

Where is your observer writing from?
Think who would be more dramatic/ powerful?

Different ways of starting a sentence to add interest:

1. Provide Further Explanation (Colon)

The early morning sun shone over the river as I walked across the bridge: it was surely a sign of better things to come.

2. Start with an Action (Verb Phrase)

Running as fast as I could, I realised about halfway across the bridge that I wouldn't make in time.

3. Describe the Mood or Manner (Adverb)

Cautiously, I looked up and saw the silhouette of the building where I knew she would be waiting.

4. Convey a 'Measured' Inner-Thought (Brackets)

The bridge was almost deserted (remarkably, not a single commuter or tourist in sight) and I finally felt free.

5. Convey a 'Spontaneous' Inner-Thought (Dashes)

She said she would be there – she had been absolutely clear – so perhaps it was unfair of me of start having doubts.

6. Qualify a Statement (Subordinate Clause)

Although the sun had now broken through the early morning fog, I still felt the chill of the wind coming from the river.

7. Change Direction (Subordinate Clause)

The light on the river was clear and bright, but my future remained cloudy.

8. Ask a Question (Rhetorical Question)

Why wasn't anyone taking the time to appreciate the beautiful morning light?

9. Repeat an Image (Repetition)

The light on the river was golden. My future was golden. Everything had worked out exactly as I had planned.

Language devices:

- ALLITERATION
- ADJECTIVES
- ADVERBS
- METAPHORS
- ONOMATOPOEIA
- PERSONIFICATION
- SIMILES
- EMOTIVE LANGUAGE
- RHETORICAL QUESTIONS
- SIBILANCE
- JUXAPOSITION
- PUNCTUATION
- SENSORY IMAGERY
- VARIED SENTENCE STRUCTURE
- IMAGERY
- FIGURATIVE LANGUAGE

Advice:

1. You can box 3-5 different parts of the picture to help with organising ideas, for example:

2. Plan your introduction and conclusion.
3. Add in your main points for each paragraph.
4. Decide on an order for your paragraphs

5. Think where you might use certain language features or structures.
6. Number your paragraphs once you have planned to decide on an effective structure.

5 MINUTE PLAN:

- Narrative perspective
- ATMOSPHERE
- WHO
- WHAT
- WHERE
- WHY
- WHEN
- QUICK CHARACTERS
- START POINT
- END POINT

Add contrast between different things

Sample Answer:

Write a description as suggested by this picture:

The sun sank lower in the clouds, casting a warm golden glow over the river and the majestic bridge that stood tall in the centre. As the cars patiently crawled forward in the early evening traffic, a gentle hum filled the air, resembling the distant harmonies of an orchestra tuning their instruments.

Shafts of light danced playfully between the people as they gracefully moved across the bridge, their figures casting long shadows on the ground. Each person seemed to be captivated by the enchanting scene, occasionally pausing to soak in the breathtaking beauty that enveloped them. The bridge, an architectural masterpiece, appeared to stretch on forever, its elegant curves blending harmoniously with the natural surroundings.

A gentle breeze swept through, rustling the leaves of the trees that lined the riverbank, adding a soothing soundtrack to the symphony of sights. Passionate hues of orange and red adorned the sky, painting a picturesque backdrop against which the bridge stood proudly. The water below flowed calmly, its surface mirroring the brilliance of the setting sun, creating a peaceful oasis amidst the chaos of city life.

As the tired commuters made their way home, some with weary faces, their eyes were inevitably drawn to the shimmering reflection of the bridge on the water. It was as if the bridge held a secret, a tale waiting to be unravelled. People from all walks of life crossed its path, musing upon the stories it could tell if only its stones could speak.

The bridge, a silent witness to countless moments of joy and sorrow, stood as a symbol of connection. It united the bustling city on one side with the tranquil beauty of nature on the other, bridging the gap between the man-made and the natural world. It was a testament to mankind's ingenuity and determination, a physical manifestation of the human desire to explore and conquer.

Features of the sample answer:

1. **Sensory Language:** The use of descriptive language engages the reader's senses, bringing the scene to life. For example, "A gentle breeze swept through, rustling the leaves" appeals to the sense of touch and sound, while "Passionate hues of orange and red adorned the sky" appeals to the sense of sight.

2. **Figurative Language:** Figurative language, such as similes and metaphors, enhances the descriptive quality of the text. For instance, "Shafts of light danced playfully between the people" uses the metaphor of light dancing to create a vivid image in the reader's mind.

3. **Varied Sentence Structure:** The text incorporates a variety of sentence structures, including long and short sentences, to create rhythm and maintain the reader's interest. For example, the sentence "The bridge, an architectural masterpiece....... natural surroundings" utilizes a long sentence structure to emphasize the bridge's grandeur.

4. **Imagery:** The use of vivid imagery paints a clear picture in the reader's mind. For instance, "Passionate hues of orange and red adorned the sky, painting a picturesque backdrop against which the bridge stood proudly" creates a vivid mental image of the colourful sky against the bridge.

5. **Emotional Appeal:** The text captures the emotions of the characters, such as their captivation by the beauty of the scene and their sense of wonder. This appeals to the reader's emotions, making the writing more engaging and relatable.

Write a description of travelling as suggested by this picture:

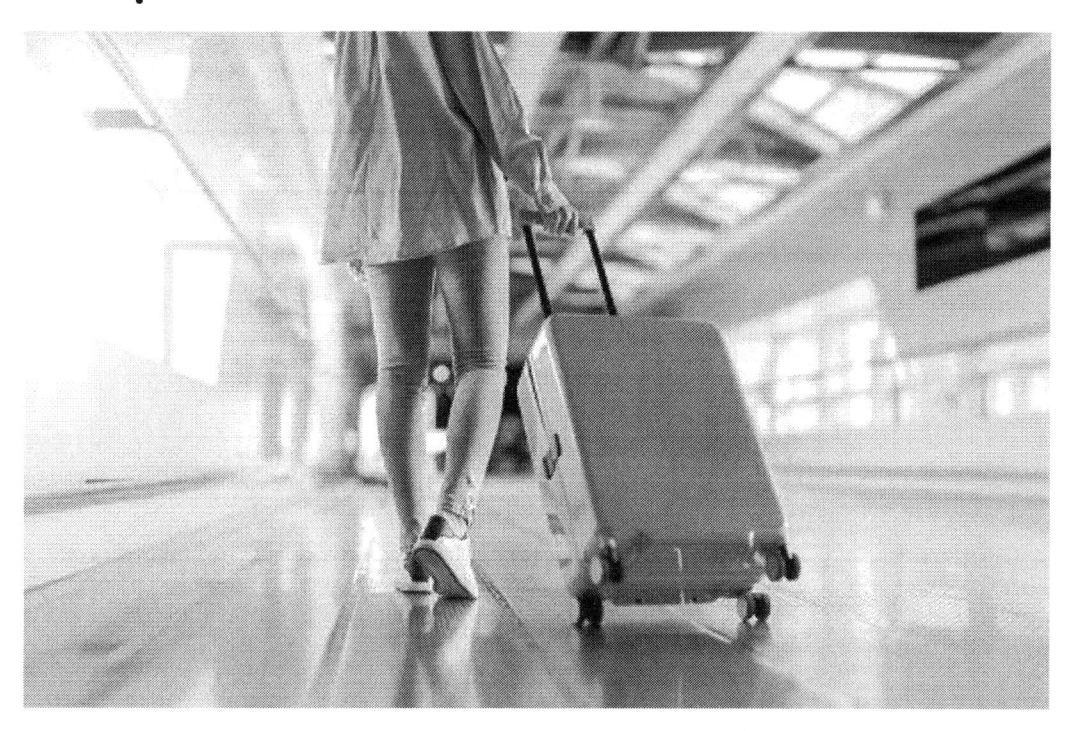

Travelling abroad is an exhilarating experience that fills your senses with awe and wonder. From the captivating sights to the enticing aromas, every moment leaves an indelible impression on your memory.

Use some of the ideas below as prompts for your descriptive writing:

1. The bustling streets filled with vibrant shops and colourful stalls...
2. The magnificent architecture of ancient temples and palaces...
3. The tranquil beauty of sandy beaches and crystal-clear waters...
4. The enchanting aroma of freshly brewed coffee and warm pastries...
5. The resplendent scenery of rolling hills and blooming meadows...
6. The captivating sound of laughter and music echoing through lively squares...
7. The breathtaking sight of snow-capped mountains against the clear blue sky...
8. The bustling atmosphere of lively markets and bustling bazaars...
9. The idyllic charm of quaint villages nestled amidst lush greenery...
10. The striking contrast of modern skyscrapers against a backdrop of historic landmarks...

Planning sheet

Sensory detail:

Sight []
Sound []
Smell []
Touch []
Taste []

Atmosphere and tone	Different sentence starters
Similes/metaphor/personification	
Start point	End point

Write a description as suggested by this picture:

Use some of the ideas below as prompts for your descriptive writing:

1. The mountains rise like ancient giants, their peaks covered in a light dusting of snow.
2. The quiet lapping of the water against the wooden pier fills the air, creating a soothing soundtrack to the scene.
3. The wind whispers through the valley, carrying with it a sense of serenity and tranquillity.
4. Occasionally, the sound of a distant waterfall can be heard, adding to the enchanting ambiance of the pier.
5. The scent of wildflowers hangs in the air, sweet like the kisses of a summer breeze.
6. The lake sparkles like a thousand diamonds, its surface shimmering in the sunlight.

Planning sheet

Sensory detail:

Sight []
Sound []
Smell []
Touch []
Taste []

Atmosphere and tone	Different sentence starters
Similes/metaphor/personification	
Start point	End point

Write a description of an idyllic location as suggested by this picture:

Use some of the ideas below as prompts for your descriptive writing:

1. A serene oasis...

2. A tranquil haven surrounded by nature...

3. An enchanting world of cascading waterfalls and lush greenery...

4. A breathtaking paradise with crystal-clear turquoise waters...

5. A picturesque landscape, painted with vibrant flowers and rolling hills...

6. A peaceful sanctuary nestled amidst towering mountains and pristine lakes...

7. A radiant garden, brimming with colourful blossoms and fluttering butterflies...

8. A majestic castle, perched on a hill overlooking a scenic valley...

9. A blissful retreat, where time stands still and worries melt away...

10. A harmonious beach, where soft golden sand meets the crashing waves...

Planning sheet

Sensory detail:

Sight []
Sound []
Smell []
Touch []
Taste []

Atmosphere and tone	Different sentence starters
Similes/metaphor/personification	
Start point	End point

Write a description of a storm as suggested by this picture:

Use some of the ideas below as prompts for your descriptive writing:

1. Raindrops hammered against the window, creating a symphony of sound.
2. The storm raged with a furious intensity, lightning crackling across the sky.
3. The sky turned a foreboding shade of grey, as the storm clouds gathered ominously.
4. Through the window, the rain fell in torrents, blurring everything in its path.
5. The darkness of the storm swallowed everything in its path, leaving only shadows in its wake.
6. Flashes of lightning illuminated the landscape, revealing the chaos and destruction left by the storm.

Planning sheet

Sensory detail:

Sight []
Sound []
Smell []
Touch []
Taste []

Atmosphere and tone	Different sentence starters
Similes/metaphor/personification	
Start point	End point

Write a description of travelling in a train as suggested by this picture:

Use some of the ideas below as prompts for your descriptive writing:

1. A sleek, silver bullet...
2. The rhythmic clatter of wheels on the tracks...
3. A striking panorama of rolling hills and vast meadows...
4. A bustling carriage filled with chattering commuters...
5. The soothing hum of the engine...
6. Delicious aroma of freshly brewed coffee wafting through the air...
7. The velvety touch of plush, burgundy seats...
8. The intriguing tales of fellow travellers unfolding in hushed whispers...
9. The gentle embrace of cool air as the train glides through tunnels...
10. The carriage was filled with the earthy smell of damp soil as the train passed through a dense forest, evoking a sense of calm and tranquillity.

Planning sheet

Sensory detail:

Sight []
Sound []
Smell []
Touch []
Taste []

Atmosphere and tone	Different sentence starters
Similes/metaphor/personification	
Start point	End point

Write a description of fireworks night as suggested by this picture:

Fireworks night, also known as Bonfire Night or Guy Fawkes Night, is a spectacular celebration that takes place annually in the United Kingdom on the 5th of November. This evening event commemorates the failed Gunpowder Plot of 1605 and has become a much-anticipated tradition.

Use some of the ideas below as prompts for your descriptive writing:

1. As darkness descends, the sky transforms into a mesmerizing canvas of vibrant colours and illuminations.
2. The air crackles with a sense of excitement and anticipation as families and friends gather together to witness this dazzling display.
3. Enchanting sparklers fizzing and crackling...
4. Fiery trails of light painting the sky...
5. The striking combination of colours and patterns...
6. Radiant showers of shimmering sparks...
7. Glittering cascades of bright stars...
8. Magnificent bursts of crackling thunder...

Planning sheet

Sensory detail:

Sight []
Sound []
Smell []
Touch []
Taste []

Atmosphere and tone	Different sentence starters
Similes/metaphor/personification	
Start point	End point

Write a description of gardening as suggested by this picture:

Use some of the ideas below as prompts for your descriptive writing:

1. The garden was a sea of vibrant colours, with roses, tulips, and daisies blooming in full bloom.
2. Arrayed in perfect symmetry, the neatly trimmed hedges framed the garden like majestic sentinels.
3. The lush green grass carpeted the ground, providing a soothing contrast to the colourful flower beds.
4. As the sun dipped below the horizon, the garden came alive with a spectacle of fluttering butterflies.
5. Glistening drops of dew adorned the petals, sparkling in the morning light.

Planning sheet

Sensory detail:

Sight []
Sound []
Smell []
Touch []
Taste []

Atmosphere and tone	Different sentence starters
Similes/metaphor/personification	
Start point	End point

Write a description of a beach as suggested by this picture:

Use some of the ideas below as prompts for your descriptive writing:

1. The sand is the gentlest hue of gold, almost earthen and muted, the humble star of the scene.
2. Looking out towards the sea, the waves danced under the sunlight, creating a mesmerizing display of sparkling water.
3. The beach was a vibrant canvas of colourful beach towels, umbrellas, and families enjoying their day in the sun.
4. Close to the shore, the briny smell of seaweed washed up by the waves lingered in the air, adding a natural and earthy fragrance.

Planning sheet

Sensory detail:

Sight []
Sound []
Smell []
Touch []
Taste []

Atmosphere and tone	Different sentence starters
Similes/metaphor/personification	
Start point	End point

Write a description of a deserted house as suggested by this picture:

Use some of the ideas below as prompts for your descriptive writing:

1. Old, shredded curtains hung from windows left and right...
2. A neglected home, covered in dust and cobwebs, standing alone in the barren landscape...
3. The derelict mansion, once grand, now forgotten and decaying...
4. A haunting cottage, with its crumbling walls and creaking floorboards, nestled deep in the woods...
5. The desolate and isolated farmhouse, surrounded by miles of empty fields...
6. An abandoned and eerie building, its damp rooms filled with shattered memories...
7. A lifeless and foreboding manor, hauntingly perched on a hilltop...

Planning sheet

Sensory detail:

Sight []
Sound []
Smell []
Touch []
Taste []

Atmosphere and tone	Different sentence starters
Similes/metaphor/personification	
Start point	End point

Write a description of a busy city as suggested by this picture:

Use some of the ideas below as prompts for your descriptive writing:

1. A cacophony of honking horns...
2. A sea of rushing pedestrians...
3. An amalgamation of smells and sounds...
4. A tapestry of cultures and experiences...
5. The rhythm of footsteps and chatter...
6. A symphony of car engines and sirens...
7. A myriad of shimmering lights...
8. A whirlwind of activity...
9. A labyrinth of winding streets...
10. A sensory overload of sights and sounds...

Planning sheet

Sensory detail:

Sight []
Sound []
Smell []
Touch []
Taste []

Atmosphere and tone	Different sentence starters
Similes/metaphor/personification	
Start point	End point

Write a description of a library as suggested by this picture:

Use some of the ideas below as prompts for your descriptive writing:

1. A library is an enchanting place filled with the magic of knowledge and stories.
2. It is a sanctuary where the mind can wander, exploring worlds both real and imagined.
3. The library holds the key to endless possibilities and the portal to countless adventures.
4. Within its walls, time seems to stand still as whispers of inspiration float through the air.
5. The scent of aged paper and ink mingled in the air, conjuring memories of generations past.
6. The subtle fragrance of slightly musty books added a touch of nostalgia to the library's atmosphere.
7. The rhythmic turning of pages and the occasional hushed whisper created a soothing symphony of the library's ambiance.
8. A gentle murmur of whispered conversations among avid readers could be heard, adding to the atmosphere of concentration.

Planning sheet

Sensory detail:

Sight []
Sound []
Smell []
Touch []
Taste []

Atmosphere and tone	Different sentence starters
Similes/metaphor/personification	
Start point	End point

Write a description about studying as suggested by this picture:

Use some of the ideas below as prompts for your descriptive writing:

1. A neat and tidy work area...
2. An organized desk with all the study materials in place...
3. A cluttered workspace filled with textbooks, notebooks, and stationery...
4. A serene table positioned near a window overlooking nature...
5. A quiet corner with comfortable seating and a dedicated study desk...
6. A cozy workstation adorned with motivational posters and personal mementos...
7. A well-lit area with a sleek and ergonomic writing surface...
8. An isolated spot free from distraction for focused learning...
9. A peaceful study nook tucked away in the library...
10. An inviting study setup with a supportive chair and a well-placed reading lamp...

Planning sheet

Sensory detail:

Sight []

Sound []

Smell []

Touch []

Taste []

Atmosphere and tone	Different sentence starters
Similes/metaphor/personification	
Start point	End point

Write a description of climbing as suggested by this picture:

Use some of the ideas below as prompts for your descriptive writing:

1. Climbing a mountain with someone can be an exhilarating and breathtaking experience.
2. The rugged peaks, steep slopes, and majestic valleys offer a stunning backdrop for anyone seeking an adventure of a lifetime.
3. With a mix of excitement, determination, and a touch of trepidation, the ascent begins, each step bringing you closer to the summit.
4. A symphony of bird songs filled the air, harmonizing with our footsteps as we climbed higher.
5. The rustling of leaves created a melodious melody, providing a soundtrack to our adventure.
6. The rough texture of the rock offered a reassuring grip as we carefully traversed the treacherous path.
7. The mountain peak rose above the horizon like a mighty king surveying its kingdom.
8. The cliffs were like giant sentinels guarding the secrets of the wilderness.

Planning sheet

Sensory detail:

Sight []
Sound []
Smell []
Touch []
Taste []

Atmosphere and tone	Different sentence starters
Similes/metaphor/personification	
Start point	End point

Write a description of an enjoyable meal as suggested by this picture:

Use some of the ideas below as prompts for your descriptive writing:

1. A steaming plate of succulent barbequed ribs…
2. A tower of fluffy pancakes drizzled with maple syrup…
3. A generous bowl of creamy mushroom soup…
4. A platter of sizzling stir-fried vegetables with noodles…
5. A slice of freshly baked apple pie with a dollop of vanilla ice cream…
6. A fragrant cup of spiced chai tea with a hint of cinnamon…
7. A tender, juicy steak cooked to perfection…
8. A basket of warm, crusty bread rolls…
9. A vibrant salad bursting with ripe tomatoes, crisp lettuce, and tangy dressing…
10. A silky-smooth chocolate mousse topped with shaved dark chocolate…

Planning sheet

Sensory detail:

Sight []
Sound []
Smell []
Touch []
Taste []

Atmosphere and tone	Different sentence starters
Similes/metaphor/personification	
Start point	End point

Write a description of a remote village as suggested by this picture:

Use some of the ideas below as prompts for your descriptive writing:

1. The remote village stood atop a hill, its quaint cottages huddled together in a mesmerizing dance of colours.
2. The vibrant flowers lining the cobblestone streets added a delightful burst of colour to the otherwise tranquil scenery.
3. Standing at the village's edge, I marvelled at the breathtaking sunset, painting the sky with hues of gold and crimson.
4. The village's charm, like a comforting blanket, enveloped all who visited, offering solace and tranquillity.
5. The cobblestone streets, worn smooth as whispers, whispered tales of bygone eras.
6. Crisp, autumn air wrapped around the village like a comforting embrace, invigorating all who breathed it.
7. The scent of freshly baked bread hung in the air like a warm, inviting hug from a loved one.
8. The village's silence, broken only by the gentle rustle of leaves, was a balm to the soul.

Planning sheet

Sensory detail:

Sight []
Sound []
Smell []
Touch []
Taste []

Atmosphere and tone	Different sentence starters
Similes/metaphor/personification	
Start point	End point

Write a description of the moon as suggested by this picture:

Use some of the ideas below as prompts for your descriptive writing:

1. The soft rustle of leaves seemed to harmonize with the moon's celestial hum, creating a soothing melody.
2. The sound of silence enveloped me, as if the moon had hushed everything around to savour its own serenity.
3. The air tasted crisp and pure, as though the moon's ethereal essence had been distilled into every breath.
4. There was a subtle metallic tang in the air, reminiscent of the moon's silver glow against the darkened sky.
5. The moon shimmered like a pearl in the vast velvet sky.
6. The moon glowed as bright as the guiding star, leading lost souls home.
7. The moon hung in the night sky like a delicate silver lantern, casting a soft glow over the world.
8. Like a silent guardian, the moon's ancient face watched over the sleeping Earth, its mysteries hidden in plain sight.
9. The moon, a radiant queen of the night sky, cast its enchanting spell on all who dared to look up.

Planning sheet

Sensory detail:

Sight []
Sound []
Smell []
Touch []
Taste []

Atmosphere and tone	Different sentence starters
Similes/metaphor/personification	
Start point	End point

Write a description of a party as suggested by this picture:

Use some of the ideas below as prompts for your descriptive writing:

1. Illuminated by glittering fairy lights, the dance floor seemed to come alive with vibrant colours.
2. A sea of enthusiastic partygoers, dressed in dazzling costumes, filled the room.
3. From the corner of my eye, I noticed a cascade of confetti showering the air like a magical rain.
4. The room was transformed into a whirlwind of motion, with twirling dancers captivating everyone's gaze.
5. The decorations, a harmonious blend of vivid hues and shimmering accents, caught my eye as they gleamed in the moonlight.
6. The DJ's beats were like a magnetic force, pulling everyone to the dance floor.
7. The room was a kaleidoscope of colours, spinning and blending in a mesmerizing dance.
8. Her smile lit up the room, shining like a thousand stars on a clear summer night.
9. The crowd surged forward, a tidal wave of excitement, ready to embrace the night.

Planning sheet

Sensory detail:

Sight []
Sound []
Smell []
Touch []
Taste []

Atmosphere and tone	Different sentence starters
Similes/metaphor/personification	
Start point	End point

Write a description of a barbecue as suggested by this picture:

Use some of the ideas below as prompts for your descriptive writing:

1. The crackling sound of the barbecue filled the air, accompanied by occasional pops.
2. Sizzling meat released a symphony of scrumptious sounds, enticing everyone nearby.
3. The gentle hiss of burger patties hitting the hot grill resonated through the garden.
4. Laughter and chatter filled the atmosphere as friends and family gathered around the barbecue.
5. The smoky flavour of the barbecued chicken wings was as intense as a roaring bonfire.
6. The tenderness of the grilled steak was as delicate as a melting snowflake.
7. The aroma of the sizzling prawns permeated the air like a fragrant symphony.
8. The heat radiating from the sizzling grill was as scorching as a blazing summer sun.

Planning sheet

Sensory detail:

Sight []
Sound []
Smell []
Touch []
Taste []

Atmosphere and tone	Different sentence starters
Similes/metaphor/personification	
Start point	End point

Write a description of a concert as suggested by this picture:

Use some of the ideas below as prompts for your descriptive writing:

1. Illuminated by a dazzling array of multi-coloured lights, the stage came alive with energy.
2. The fog machine engulfed the performers, creating an otherworldly atmosphere.
3. The crowd swayed in unison, their arms raised, creating a beautiful sea of movement.
4. Strobe lights flickered in time with the music, casting dramatic shadows on the performers.
5. The fireworks exploded above the stage, showering the audience with a cascade of sparkling colours.
6. As the guitarist strummed the first chord, a wave of applause erupted from the audience.
7. The drums thundered, shaking the ground beneath our feet and instilling a sense of urgency.
8. The faint hint of sweat and adrenaline lingered, a testament to the passion of the performers.
9. The singer's voice was as smooth as velvet, caressing our ears with each note.

Planning sheet

Sensory detail:

Sight []
Sound []
Smell []
Touch []
Taste []

Atmosphere and tone	Different sentence starters
Similes/metaphor/personification	
Start point	End point

Write a description of woodland as suggested by this picture:

Use some of the ideas below as prompts for your descriptive writing:

1. Through the maze of ancient trees, sunlight creates a mesmerizing play of shadows.
2. A vibrant tapestry of wildflowers adorns the woodland, painting it with a myriad of colours.
3. The towering ancient oak trees stretch their branches towards the heavens, casting a majestic silhouette against the sky.
4. Sunlight filters through the dense canopy, creating a resplendent, dappled glow on the woodland floor.
5. The haunting melody of the hidden stream dances through the woodland, serenading its visitors.
6. Rustling foliage and whispering branches carry the secrets of the woodland on the gentle breeze.
7. The hushed footsteps of woodland creatures create a sense of deep tranquillity.
8. The woodland was a tranquil oasis amidst the chaos of city life.

Planning sheet

Sensory detail:

Sight []
Sound []
Smell []
Touch []
Taste []

Atmosphere and tone	Different sentence starters
Similes/metaphor/personification	
Start point	End point

Printed in Great Britain
by Amazon